Lincoln School Library

CRACK

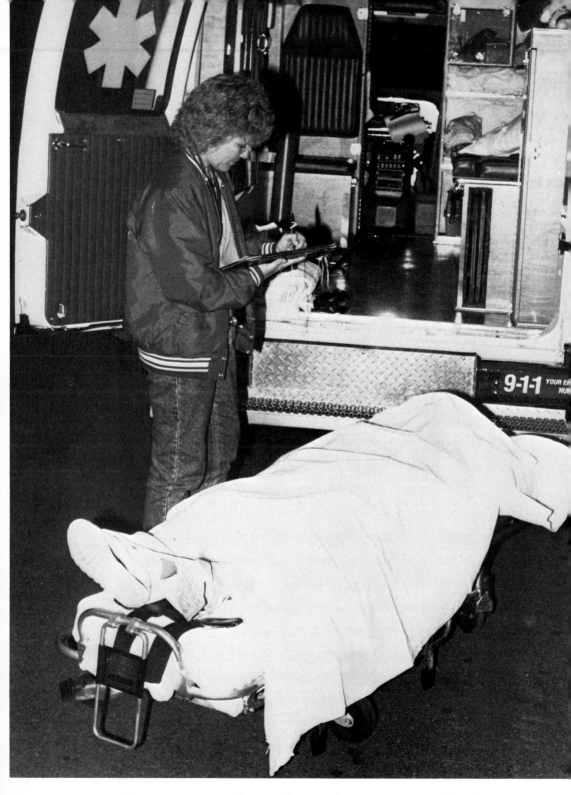

Teenagers may overdose on drugs without meaning to. Then they become accident statistics.

THE DRUG ABUSE PREVENTION LIBRARY

CRACK

Rodney G. Peck

The Rosen Publishing Group, Inc.
New York

Published in 1991, 1993, 1997, 2000 by the
Rosen Publishing Group, Inc.
29 East 21st Street, New York, NY 10010

Copyright © 1991, 1993, 1997, 2000 by the Rosen
Publishing Group, Inc.

Revised Edition 2000

Library of Congress Cataloging-in-Publication Data

Peck, Rodney G.
  Crack / Rodney G. Peck
  (The drug abuse prevention library)
  Includes bibliographical references and index.
  Summary: Discusses the characteristics of crack cocaine
    and the dangers of using the drug.
  ISBN 0-8239-3312-1
  1. Crack (Drug)—Juvenile literature. 2. Cocaine habit—
    Juvenile literature. [1. Crack (Drug). 2. Cocaine habit.
    3. Drug abuse.]
    I. Title. II. Series.
  HV5809.5.P43 1991
  362.29'8—dc20   91-11141
                                    CIP
                                     AC

Manufactured in the United States of America

Contents

Teenagers sometimes try drugs just because they are forbidden.

The Road to Dependence

In the late 1980s and early 1990s, a number of Hollywood movies attempted to show some of the harsh and ugly realities of American city life. These movies include *New Jack City, King of New York,* and *Jungle Fever.* Something these movies all had in common was their attempt to show the negative consequences of America's recent obsession with the drug cocaine, particularly in its most addictive form: crack. They showed all the filth and disgrace of the crackhead's life—the hellish crackhouses where addicts buy and use the drug; prostitution, theft, and crime; family neglect and abuse; gang violence; neighborhoods torn apart.

The problem was that many viewers

8 | thought that the movies showed events of a time that had passed and that cocaine was not a concern anymore. After all, it was in the mid-1980s that use of cocaine hit its peak use in the United States. In the late 1970s and early 1980s, cocaine was seen as a hip and harmless recreational drug. At the time, most people were fooled into believing that cocaine was not addictive.

The problem, of course, is that cocaine is very addictive. And by the mid-1980s, drug dealers had developed and were selling cocaine in an even more addictive form: as crack. Crack is cocaine that has been specially processed to be sold in very small doses, called rocks, and is smoked rather than snorted. Because it is smoked, crack gets into the bloodstream very quickly and is very addictive. Indeed, some experts believe that crack is the most addictive substance known to humankind. By the mid-1980s, an estimated six million Americans, the highest number in the country's history, were regular users. And the resulting damage was easy to see: addiction, arrests, violence, a long list of tragedy and sorrow.

So when movies like *Jungle Fever* and *New Jack City* came out, many Americans believed that the country had learned its

lesson. After all, by 1991, cocaine use had | **9**
reached its lowest level in decades. Just
1.2 million Americans were still regularly
using cocaine. It was hoped that Americans
had learned their lessons about the dangers
of cocaine and crack use.

And maybe they had. Since 1991,
cocaine and crack use in the United
States has remained at about the same
level. But there is one group in which
cocaine and crack use has increased a lot
in the past couple of years: young people,
specifically teenagers. First-time use of
cocaine and crack among teens is at its
highest level since the 1980s. Maybe it's
time for a little refresher course about this
very dangerous drug.

Tolerance and Dependence

Tolerance is part of the process that
leads to dependence and addiction. The
human body is constantly changing. When
a person begins using or experimenting
with drugs, the body adapts to them. Over
time—and for teens it's a relatively short
period of time—the body needs more of
the drug for the user to feel the same
effects. This is because your body gets
used to the drug, and it builds up a tolerance to it. Over time, that tolerance

10 | develops into dependence, which means your body has changed so that you don't just need the drug to get high, you need it to feel normal. When you reach this stage, you are dependent on that drug.

Dependence has both a physical and a psychological part to it. In psychological terms, dependence means that a user simply does not feel "right" or "normal" when he or she is not using the drug. Without the drug, the person may experience symptoms such as anxiety or depression. In physical terms, dependence means that the person experiences a range of sometimes severe physical symptoms when he or she stops using the drug. Such symptoms, which are known as withdrawal, include fever, bodyache, and other flulike symptoms; fatigue; tremors and shaking; vomiting and diarrhea. In rare and extreme cases, withdrawal can even cause death.

Addiction: A Disease

The disease of addiction is the final stage of drug use. Addicted people live for their drug. They think of almost nothing but their next high.

Doctors and scientists recognize addiction as a disease. Because it is a disease, overcoming addiction usually requires medical treatment.

It is widely believed that addiction is a complex combination of physical, emotional, and environmental factors. That is why the most successful treatment includes a combination of short-term and long-term therapy.

Drug dependence and addiction can happen to anyone. But for some people, addiction to drugs is more likely than for other people.

Studies show that the family members of drug addicts are more likely to become addicts than people without drug addicts in their family. If you have the disease of drug addiction in your family, be aware of the dangerous situation you put yourself in if you decide to use drugs. Any experimenting is a risk.

Crack is a dangerous drug. In this book you will read about how crack is made and what it can do to your body. You will learn about how crack hurts everybody, not just users. You will also learn how young people often start using crack after experimenting with drugs they think are less harmful, such as alcohol and tobacco. You will find out ways to avoid starting down the road to drug dependence.

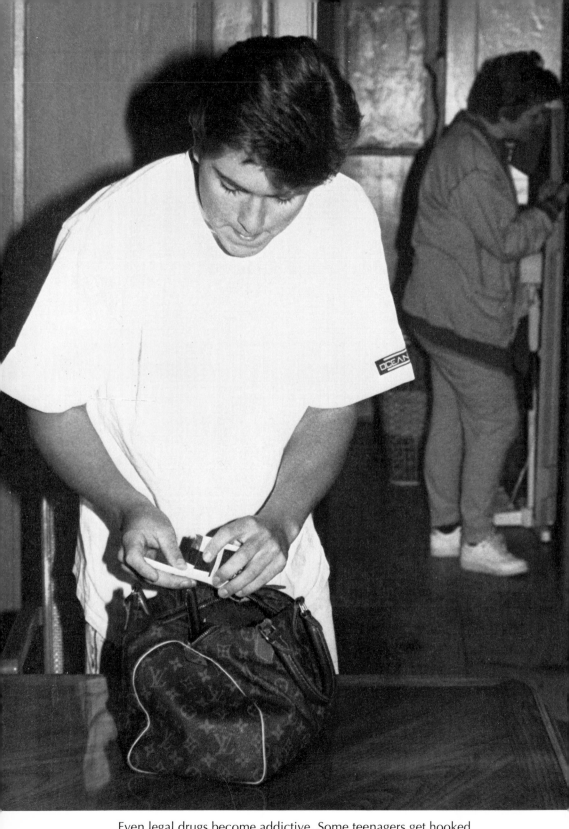

Even legal drugs become addictive. Some teenagers get hooked on cigarettes.

CHAPTER 2

Where Drug Problems Begin

In all states, it is against the law for a person under twenty-one years of age to drink alcohol. It is also against the law for a person under eighteen to buy cigarettes. Many teenagers choose to ignore these laws, and drug use starts for many people when they are teens. And it usually starts with drugs such as alcohol and tobacco.

Because alcohol and tobacco are legal for adults, they are easy to get. And according to the U.S. Department of Justice, so is marijuana. They claim that 90 percent of high school seniors report that they could obtain marijuana "very or fairly easily." Young people may get these drugs from older brothers and sisters.

14   They get them from friends. They also get them from their parent's liquor cabinet or private stash.

The big question is: "Why do young people take drugs?" This is what some young people say:

"I just want to forget my problems."

Danielle got drunk for the first time because she wanted to forget about a fight she had with her boyfriend. She took her parents' car and got into an accident. Getting drunk caused her more problems in the end.

"I want to be cool."

There is nothing cool about damaging your brain or being so wasted that you can't remember where you've been or what you've done. Take a closer look at people who use crack. There is nothing cool about lying and stealing to buy another hit.

"My older sister and her friends do it."

Watson felt like everyone treated him like a child. He wanted to look and act mature like his older sister Mai. One night during a party when a friend of his sister's offered him a crack pipe, he tried it. His heart pounded so hard he felt sick and had to leave the party.

"I'm sick of my parents telling me what to do."

Using drugs to rebel can hurt your parents a great deal. But remember, it also hurts the people who take the drug. And sometimes it can even kill them. Taking drugs to rebel or to show anger hurts everybody and adds to your stress.

"My friends are using it."

Sometimes it's really hard to say no to a friend. But a true friend won't force you to do something you don't want to do. People can be either leaders or followers. You can be a leader instead of agreeing to go along with something that could get all of you in trouble. Suggest fun things to do. You don't have to do anything just because your friends do it.

"I like the feeling of getting high."

What kinds of things do you like to do? Seeing a funny movie can give you a good feeling. Spending time with friends or playing sports can give you good feelings. Many things in life make you feel good. Try concentrating on those things instead

16   of risking your health and your future by using drugs.

"I want to be popular."

Derek and Juan both were popular. Juan used drugs, but Derek didn't. One day Juan got caught with cocaine in his locker. He was suspended from school and taken to juvenile court. The story was on the local news. Now, he's well-known for being a drug user, not for being a good person. Derek is popular for being good at sports, and for being nice and funny. His popularity is based on qualities that will last.

"I was curious about drugs."

Why be curious? You know that drugs can hurt or kill you. You wouldn't stand in front of a train to see how it would feel if it hit you. You know what would happen. Fast-moving trains and drugs are both dangerous. Both can kill you. It doesn't make sense to play with either one.

"It can't happen to me."

Wrong! Almost every day we hear about people who have lost their jobs, their families, or their future because of drug use. Kids are kicked out of school for

Smoking and drinking are part of the party scene.

18 using, possessing, or selling drugs. People die. It happens to others. But it can happen to you if you choose to use drugs.

Ask any addict if he or she is happy to be an addict. Nobody takes drugs wanting to become addicted. Everyone who is an addict once thought, "It can't happen to me." And now their lives are a mess.

Gateway Drugs and Growing Bodies

No drug, whether legal or illegal, is perfectly safe. And in several important ways, drugs are more dangerous for teens than they are for adults. This is true even for drugs that adults can legally use, such as alcohol and tobacco.

One reason that drug use is more dangerous for teens is that teens like to think of themselves as adults. Indeed, it is an important and natural part of teen development to experiment with adult roles and behaviors. Even so, teens have not finished growing. Emotionally, intellectually, and physically, some of your most important development takes place during your teen years and even beyond. For example, many people think you stop growing at age eighteen, but your body continues to grow and develop throughout your early twenties. The use of any kind of drug interferes with and slows all of your growth processes. Something else to keep in mind is that, physically, a growing body can become addicted to a drug ten times faster than an adult body. And because young bodies are growing so fast, they build up a tolerance to drugs much faster.

Another reason teens should be especially cautious about drugs is that statistics show that early use of any drug leads to an increased risk of problems, including addiction, later in life. Studies also seem to indicate that the use of any drug by young adults, even a lower-risk substance such as tobacco or marijuana, may increase the likelihood of a person eventually using more dangerous drugs. For this reason, some experts refer to tobacco, alcohol, and marijuana as gateway drugs, meaning that using them opens the door to using other, more dangerous drugs.

Choose the Road to a Bright Future

Many people start on the road to drug dependence when they're teenagers. They may try alcohol or cigarettes in order to look cool or fit in. They may try harder drugs, like crack, because they're curious

Many students, at all kinds of schools, face drug pressures on a daily basis. Often times teens will try drugs in a misguided effort to fit in or to look cool.

or they think everybody's doing it. These first steps can lead to addiction. Drug addicts suffer physical and mental health problems and usually end up getting in trouble with their families and the law.

You can choose to take the better road. You can avoid alcohol, marijuana, and tobacco, which can lead to trying harder drugs later. Spend your time with friends who agree that drugs are harmful.

Together, you can find fun, cool things to do that won't mess up your life.

A drug habit leads the addict to crime to get money for more crack or cocaine.

CHAPTER 3

Cocaine: Where Crack Comes From

You now know that tobacco, marijuana, and alcohol are regarded as gateway drugs, which means that oftentimes they lead to the use of harder, more dangerous substances. Cocaine is one of those more dangerous drugs.

What is cocaine? Where does it come from? Why do people take cocaine?

Cocaine is a very powerful stimulant. A stimulant makes your body work faster. It speeds up your brain and your heart. Scientists are still studying exactly how cocaine works in the body. They believe that cocaine may interfere with the way the brain processes a substance called dopamine. Dopamine is a neurotransmitter, a substance that the body's nerves

24 use to communicate with each other. Scientists think that dopamine is responsible for the feelings of pleasure that people experience. Similarly, a lack of dopamine causes feelings of depression. Cocaine confuses the way the brain and body produce and process dopamine, which explains why cocaine makes users feel "high" or euphoric at first and why, without it, they feel depressed or anxious. Basically, cocaine interferes with your body's ability to feel things normally.

There are many names for cocaine. People call it "coke," "blow," or "snow." It is a white powder that people snort up the nose to get high. Some people inject cocaine or smoke cocaine. Any way you take it, it is a very dangerous drug.

Where does cocaine come from? It comes from the coca plant. (Don't be confused. The coca plant is different from the cacao plant, which gives us cocoa beans that are used to make chocolate.) The leaves of the coca plant contain a very small amount of cocaine.

The coca plant grows on the slopes of the Andes Mountains, which are located in South America. Many coca plants are grown in the countries of Peru and Bolivia. The Incan Indians farm coca in the mountains. They pick the coca leaves and sell them.

It takes a lot of hard work to pick the leaves. The Incas chew the coca leaves to get the small amount of the drug they contain. It helps them stay awake and work more. Chewing the coca leaves is also part of their religion.

The Incas sell the coca leaves to drug dealers. The drug dealers turn the leaves into the white powder called cocaine. They do this by first mixing the coca leaves with kerosene or acid. This is called purifying. Then that mixture is put in a press or steel drum and crushed into a mash called "pasta." Then the pasta is mixed with another acid. The end product is the white powder called cocaine. Keep in mind, this means that when you take cocaine, you are also ingesting the acidic ingredients that are used to make the drug.

But the story does not end there. Other things are added to the cocaine before it is sold to the user who buys it on the street. Drug dealers add sugar, heroin, baby powder, or other drugs to the cocaine. The buyer never knows what he or she is getting. This is just one more risk that the buyer must consider.

26   Cocaine is not a new drug in the United States. It was discovered more than 100 years ago. Scientists were searching for new medicines. They learned that the Incas chewed the leaves for energy. They also found that purifying the coca leaves gave them the strong drug called cocaine. Scientists thought that it was a safe cure for some illnesses. But many people became addicted to cocaine and many more died from it.

People decided that cocaine was not harmless. In 1906 a law was passed that limited the use of cocaine in medicines. However, cocaine can be used as a pain-killer (anesthetic) in certain operations on the nose and throat. It makes the skin numb. Only special doctors are allowed to use cocaine in very small amounts for operations.

Cocaine is a strong and dangerous drug. People can become dependent on it after one-time use. The drug dealer knows this fact. A drug-dependent person will usually do anything and pay any price to get the high. A dealer may charge a user anywhere from $45 to $100 for a single gram of cocaine. Often the dealer will give cocaine to teens for free at first.

Cocaine is expensive: A few hits cost a lot of dollars.

If a kid takes it and becomes addicted, the dealer has a new customer. Then he can charge the kid high prices for the coke.

For many years cocaine was not a problem in the United States. In 1914 it became against the law. Then the drug went on a long vacation. The public stopped using it because it was not safe.

28   When the 1980s came along, cocaine was very expensive and often referred to as the "champagne of drugs." Most people couldn't afford it, which meant cocaine was a drug for rich, trendy people. Movie stars, rock stars, and athletes were using cocaine. Sadly, even today, many celebrities suffer from their drug use.

Scott Weiland, lead singer of the Stone Temple Pilots, checked into a drug treatment center in January 1997 after being arrested for possession of cocaine and heroin. His drug treatment forced the popular band to cancel its concert tour, and they almost broke up. Since then, Weiland has had several relapses. He has been in and out of treatment centers and has been arrested again.

Actor Robert Downey Jr. is another young celebrity whose career has been affected by drug problems. In June 1996, Downey was arrested for driving under the influence, possession of a controlled substance (crack cocaine, powder cocaine, and black-tar heroin), and possession of a concealed weapon. In November 1996, he was sentenced to three years probation related to these charges.

Although Downey was able to continue on with his career, his drug addiction continued to haunt him. In 1998, he served a short prison sentence for drug possession. After his release, he spoke publicly about his struggles with the disease and his determination to beat it, but in 1999 he was arrested once again for drug-related offenses and sent back to prison.

Talented athletes, like Darryl Strawberry of the New York Yankees baseball team, have fallen as well. Strawberry has suffered several arrests, numerous suspensions—including the entire 2000 season—and marital and financial problems. Though he has experienced athletic success, his drug problems have hampered him in fulfilling his athletic potential.

These stars suffered career problems and legal trouble because of their drug use. But drugs can do more than mess up your life; they can kill you. River Phoenix was a talented young actor, but he had problems with drugs. On October 31, 1993, he died after taking cocaine with several other drugs. He was only twenty-three years old.

When police identify a crack house the dealers and buyers are hauled off to jail.

Crack and Freebasing: Very Dangerous

Snorting cocaine up your nose is not the only way to take it. Drug dealers have invented ways to change the cocaine powder so that users can smoke it. These forms of the drug are called crack and freebase.

The fastest high comes from crack. It is the most addictive form of cocaine. The craving an addict has for it is greater than for any other drug, even heroin. Some experts believe that someone can become addicted to crack the first time he or she uses it.

Crack is made by mixing cocaine with baking soda and water and then boiling it into a paste and leaving it to harden. The result is a "cookie," or mass of crack, that

32 is chipped into "rocks," which are sold to the user, ready to smoke. It's called crack because of the crackling sound it makes when smoked.

The dealers can sell a rock for $10 or $20 apiece. Almost anyone can afford to get high on crack, even younger people. This is one of the reasons its use has become so widespread. But the consequences of using crack are extremely destructive and horrific. The price you ultimately pay is your health, your dreams, or even your life.

Freebasing is another way to smoke cocaine. In freebasing, powdered cocaine is mixed with ether (a liquid that is also used as a painkiller) and other chemicals. It is very dangerous because it too is very addictive and destructive. An added danger that freebasing presents is that the ether can catch fire very easily. Many people have been badly burned or have even died while preparing to freebase.

Freebasing causes hallucinations—you see things that aren't really there. It also causes paranoia—you think the world is out to get you. And the risk to your health is very great. Freebasing can cause heart attacks or strokes. It injures your lungs, your brain, your heart, your future.

Why Is Crack So Harmful?

What is so special about crack? Why is it getting so much attention? There are many reasons. It is considered the most addictive drug known to humankind. Crack destroys families. Thousands of crack babies are born each year. There are many more reasons. Let's look at these reasons more closely.

You know that crack is cheap. It is sold on the streets, ready to smoke. You can buy it almost everywhere. That is why crack is often called the "fast food of drugs."

You also know that thousands of people are addicted to crack. They buy a lot of it. And addicts always want more. So the drug dealers need to buy more

34 cocaine to make the crack. They buy it from drug traffickers. Peru and Bolivia still lead the world in the growth of coca, although farmers in Colombia are now beginning to grow a lot as well. Previously, Colombia was the country where the raw coca grown in other places was processed for sale and shipment around the world, especially to the United States. But today, Colombia grows much of its own coca, and the cocaine trade is a very important part of its economy.

A single hit of crack costs less than a single hit of powder cocaine. A rock of crack costs between $10 and $20. Cocaine is sold in grams. A gram costs between $45 and $150. The low price of crack makes it affordable for just about anybody to buy.

But what is the real cost? Crack smokers get high and then "crash." Users want more crack to get over the depression they feel. They have to spend another $10 or $20 to get more crack. If they buy crack ten times in a week, they've spent between $100 and $200. Powder cocaine seems to cost more than crack. But, in the end, crack costs more because the users need more of it.

Crack makes addicts faster than any other drug.

Crack began to get attention around 1985. Its low price makes it special. Almost anyone can afford a $10 piece. Crack is also special because the high is very intense. The drug is smoked in a pipe. It goes straight to the lungs and brain. People become addicted quickly. So crack became very popular. Within a few months crack was in most major cities. Now it is very easy to buy even in small cities and towns.

36   Crack is also special because the dealers are very well organized. They have set up special houses for their customers. The houses are called "crack houses." The dealers sell crack in these houses. The users also smoke crack in these houses. It gives them a place to go and get high. They don't have to take a chance of getting caught on the street. They also don't have to do it at home. The crack houses are very handy for users.

Cocaine powder is snorted up the nose. Some of it is absorbed by the body. It takes the drug three or four minutes to reach the brain. Crack is different here too. It is smoked, as you know. But crack reaches the lungs and brain in *less than 10 seconds*. Whereas cocaine takes a few minutes, crack takes only a few seconds.

Cocaine powder will keep you high for two or three *hours*. Crack will keep you high for only five or ten *minutes*. The crack high is followed by a big low. The user becomes very depressed. The user feels sad and alone. The depression is hard to endure. The user buys another rock of crack and smokes it to forget the depression. That is how people become addicted so quickly. As soon as they crash, they want to get high again.

Because it is smoked, crack is stronger than powder cocaine. The strength of crack makes it very addictive, ten times more addictive than powder cocaine. Some users say that they were hooked by the first or second hit. Crack is considered the most addictive drug known to man.

People can overdose on crack at any time. Some people believe that the fact that they have developed a tolerance for a drug means that their body is better able to "handle" it and that they are at less of a risk of an overdose than a new user. Nothing could be farther from the truth, particularly when it comes to crack and cocaine.

With regard to the dangers of overdosing, these drugs are very unpredictable. Although users do develop a tolerance, they can also, at the same time, develop an increased sensitivity to certain properties of crack and cocaine, in particular those that cause convulsions. One result is that an overdose often occurs after the user has taken a normal, or even small dose. A deadly overdose can also occur with the first use.

Deadly Consequences
Scientists recently discovered a very

38 deadly example of drug interaction in an extremely common type of combination drug use: cocaine and alcohol.

Researchers found that when cocaine and alcohol are used together, the body changes them to another substance called cocaethylene, which is more toxic and dangerous than either cocaine or alcohol individually. Cocaine and alcohol is the

A crack house is sealed up after a raid so that it cannot go back into business.

two-drug combination most likely to
result in death. But the dangers of drug
use are not just limited to physical
dangers for the user.

Crack hurts everybody. Since it hit the
streets, crime has gone way up. Crack users
steal to get money to buy their drug.
Teenagers sell drugs or even their bodies
for sex to make money to buy crack.

People on crack feel as if they can take
on the world. They feel powerful and get
angry over little things. Often they become
violent. Violence is also connected to the
gangs that sell the drugs and their dangerous methods of defending their territories.

Crack dealers can make millions of
dollars. They fight over territory to get
more customers. In many cities, street
gangs and organized crime groups
compete for control of the drug trade.

Clearly, drugs are a big reason for higher
crime rates. At the end of the 1990s, U.S.
Department of Justice statistics showed
than one-third of prison inmates were
under the influence of drugs when they
committed the crime that put them behind
bars. Almost 80 percent had used drugs
regularly at some point in their life.

Law enforcement takes crack use very
seriously. Because it is so addictive and

40 | dangerous, crack is treated much more harshly in the legal system than cocaine. In the United States, crack is treated up to twenty times more severely than cocaine when it comes to arrest and sentencing.

But the tragedy doesn't stop there. In the late 1980s, it was estimated that as many as 170,000 crack babies were being born in the United States each year. A crack baby is a child born addicted to crack because his or her mother smoked crack while she was pregnant. At the time, these babies were referred to as the "lost generation" because it was believed that they were doomed to a life of severe health problems and learning difficulties that science and medicine couldn't do anything about.

Today, that prediction is much less severe. Medical evidence shows that most of these babies recover well and that their overall growth and development generally fall within the range of what is considered normal. This is not to say that using crack while you are pregnant is harmless for your baby. It does increase the likelihood that your baby will suffer from the symptoms of fetal drug syndrome. These problems can range from the short-term and relatively minor, like fussiness, restlessness, or irritability, to the long-term and irreversible like mental retardation, seizure disorders, and a host of learning disabilities and attention-deficit problems.

Child abuse and neglect have risen because of crack. Parents who use can't think about their children. They forget to feed their children. They get angry and violent with the kids more easily, too. That doesn't mean that the parents don't love their kids. It means that crack is messing up their minds. They love the high that crack gives them.

Things to Remember

Crack is smoked. It is sold on the street for a low price. Anybody can afford to buy it. All types of people smoke crack. It is ten times more powerful than powder cocaine. Anyone can overdose on crack.

Crime rates have risen because of crack. It makes people feel powerful and violent. People steal, cheat, lie, or sell their bodies for crack. It is considered the most addictive drug known to humans. Pregnant women and parents who use crack are destroying the lives of many children. That is what makes crack so harmful.

In filthy surroundings, crack addicts gather to smoke the drug in secret.

CHAPTER 6

People Who Use Crack

*F*or the last thirty years drugs have been very popular. They have a role in everyday life. Television and music videos show the exciting, fast-paced life of drinking and drug use. Some movies show young people partying, getting drunk, and getting high, making it all look fun. For years popular music has been saying that drugs are cool.

Today, many rock and rap artists sing about drugs. Nirvana, Alice in Chains, and Depeche Mode all sing about using heroin, while The Beastie Boys, Cypress Hill, and Snoop Doggy Dog openly promote smoking marijuana in their song lyrics. Many teens admire celebrities and are influenced by what they say and do. This may be one of the reasons for the increase in teen drug use.

43

44 Recent figures show that 1.5 million people in the United States use cocaine. Among young people, the rate of cocaine use is up.

Crack addiction is a big deal. Crack severely damages a person's lungs, brain, and heart. It can cause people to hallucinate and also makes people violent. Crack use has created many more problems around the world.

One recent report says that crack is so plentiful in some cities that the same vial that was $20 a few years ago now costs $3. Powdered cocaine can still cost up to $150 for one gram. In some places, crack is more affordable and accessible than ever.

Why do people use crack? Because it's available and the high is intense. One user said the high from crack is "otherworldly." Another said, "Crack is everything you expect with powder cocaine—multiplied a zillion times. And once you feel that way, you want to do it again and again."

But crack is not glamorous. "I stole, lied, cheated, and manipulated," said one crack user of her experience. Crack users sit in filthy, smelly crackhouses to get high. They sell their abused bodies for sex to buy more crack. There's nothing glamorous or mysterious about it.

Though crack costs less than other drugs, it's not as cheap as people think. A crack high lasts only five or ten minutes. The users want to get high again right away. They end up buying more, so in the end it actually costs more. The user needs more of it, more often.

Some people say that crack makes your sex life better, but repeated use of crack often causes impotence in men. That means that their penis can't get erect. Then they can't have sex at all.

Some people trade sex for crack. And the number of sexual diseases has gone up. Health workers say that sexual diseases are spreading because people are using drugs such as crack.

In time, as any crack addict will tell you, the need for crack will overcome any other drive or need that you have. It's stronger than the need for food, for water, for sex, stronger than the desire to be clean, to look good, to interact with others. That's why crack addicts present such a horrifying appearance: sickly, ragged, dirty.

When a teenager begins to neglect the important things—even eating—he may have a drug problem.

CHAPTER 7

Crack and You

*P*eople on crack change their whole lives. We know that using crack leads to crime. People steal from their family and friends. Crack users lie and cheat to get money to buy it. Other things also happen.

Drug users start hanging out with other drug users. They leave their old friends behind. Crack users lose interest in school. They don't care about work except to get money. They don't care about how they look. Drug users start dressing sloppy and not washing. They don't care about being around other people.

Crack smokers destroy their body. Your brain is the control center for your entire body. When crack affects your brain, it changes the way your eyes work. Bright light starts to hurt your eyes. Objects look fuzzy. Some crack smokers see floating objects from the corners of their eyes. Some users see little rings of light around objects. These are called "snow" lights. The crack smoker may also see two of everything.

The lungs and throat are also in trouble. Crack smoking can cause a sore throat. It can also lead to an illness called bronchitis. This makes it hard to breathe.

Smoking crack makes your body weak. Many users don't get hungry. They would rather get high than eat. So they don't eat food. Then they lose weight. The body can't fight off diseases when it is weak. That is how crack smokers get sick.

Crack users start having hallucinations. They see things that aren't there. They become paranoid. They think that everyone is out to get them. Crack also messes up your heart. It makes the heart work faster. Blood pressure goes up. Your body temperature also goes up. The body becomes weak because of the drugs. So does the heart. Using crack can make you have

a heart attack. Even young, healthy people
have heart attacks when they use crack.

Remember that crack users also get
depressed and moody without the drug.
One minute they are happy, the next, they
are mean. Crack becomes their life. They
forget about hobbies. They don't care
about school or work, family or friends.
They don't care about anything but
getting high on crack.

Many people turn to crack or other
drugs as a way of dealing with the anxiety
or depression they feel because of various
problems in their life. At first, it may
seem like drugs help, but that feeling of
relief is only the start of a vicious, sometimes deadly, downward spiral. As they
increase their drug use, the drug user is
likely to feel more anxiety or depression
because they are using. When straight, the
user is likely to recognize that using drugs
has only created a new problem. They feel
additional pain about this new problem
so they treat it by using more drugs
because that is the only way they have
learned to cope. This leads to even more
anxiety and depression, which leads to
more drug use, and so on. The cycle continues, until the user finds the strength to
stop it—or it stops them first.

Good friends and playing sports are a big help in avoiding the dangers of drugs.

CHAPTER 8

A Future Without Crack

The movies we discussed at the beginning of this book show the darkest side of drug abuse. They are fiction, but the reality of crack addiction is no less awful. The crack users in the movies are so addicted, they will do anything to get their next drug hit. They will steal, prostitute their body, or even kill to get it.

In real life, crack users do these same scary things. The drug makes them so sick that they sometimes have to be rushed to the hospital. It often makes working people lose their jobs. Crack-abusing parents are often forced to put their kids in foster care because crack keeps them from caring for the kids. These things cost the government and taxpayers money.

52 Crack is a terrible drug that affects us all, even people who don't use it.

At the time *New Jack City* was released, crime related to drug use, including crack, was at an all-time high. In the first part of the 1990s, police and the government worked so hard to fight the crack epidemic that abuse of the drug actually went down. Unfortunately, recent studies show that teen crack use is going up, along with the crime that goes with it.

One study suggested that kids today don't realize how bad crack really is. They might not think it will hurt them, so they try it, or they don't stop a friend who wants to try it. In this book you have learned that crack is extremely dangerous. It is a very powerful form of cocaine, which is a strong stimulant. It speeds up your body's systems and makes your heart work too fast and too hard. Many users die of heart failure after taking crack. Some have died after smoking crack only one time. It's clear that it's not worth risking your life to try crack.

Still, many young people try drugs like crack. There are a number of reasons why teens get involved with drugs. They may feel that taking drugs will make them look mature. Or they may be pressured by friends to try just one hit. From reading this book, you know just one hit could really mess up your life.

Ultimately, drug use is not a way of enjoying life or coping with your problems. So find things that improve your life: friendship, sports, art, books, music, family, nature, the future. And learn productive ways to deal with the problems of life.

There are many ways to avoid crack and other drugs. Hang out with people who don't do drugs and avoid places where you know drugs will be used. Most of all, be strong. Let people know how you feel about drugs. If they pressure you, tell them: "I'm not risking my life for any drug."

If you think you have a drug problem, from alcohol or tobacco to cocaine or crack, get help. Talk to an adult you trust. Be honest with them and ask them to help you get treatment. If you don't feel comfortable talking to an adult, there are places to go for help. There is a list of organizations in the back of this book that can give you more information about drug abuse and help you find a treatment program to get off drugs.

What should you do if you suspect that a friend has a drug problem? From

54 reading this book, you know the signs to look for in a crack smoker. He or she:
- changes friends
- doesn't care about work or school
- loses weight
- can't sleep
- can't concentrate
- gets angry easily
- runs out of money quickly

If you want to, you can share what you know about crack. Your friend may not have correct information. Be sure you talk when your friend is not high.

You can also be a good listener. Let your friend express feelings and tell you about problems.

There's something else you need to know. Sharing information will help. But this person needs professional help.

If you want to help your friend, don't lend money. Don't go to places where there will be drugs. Invite your friend to drug-free places.

You can also talk to your friend's parents. Let them know what you think. Don't worry about snitching on your friends. In the long run, you will be helping.

Reading this book is a great start toward avoiding the dangerous road of drug dependence. Studies show that the more young people know about the dangers of crack, the less likely they are to use it. You've learned that crack can mess up your body, damage your brain, and ruin your life—even kill you. You can choose a bright future by choosing to stay off drugs.

Glossary

anesthetic A drug that numbs pain.

anxiety Feelings of fear, worry, or uneasiness.

cocaethylene The toxic substance that forms when alcohol and cocaine are both in the user's body at the same time.

crack A highly addictive form of cocaine, made by mixing it with baking soda and water.

depression A state of feeling sad and alone.

dopamine The neurotransmitter responsible for feelings of pleasure. The "high" of cocaine is related to an excess of this substance and the following low is a result of a lack of the substance.

ether Liquid used to make freebase cocaine.

euphoric A state of extreme pleasure.

experimenting Trying something out, such as drugs, to see how they feel.

fetal drug syndrome Symptoms suffered by newborn babies whose mother used drugs during pregnancy.

freebasing The dangerous act of smoking cocaine that has been combined with ether.

gateway drugs Drugs such as alcohol, tobacco, and marijuana that can lead to the use of harder drugs, such as cocaine and crack.

hallucination Hearing, seeing, or feeling things that are not real. Can be caused by drugs like crack.

neurotransmitters Chemicals that communicate between nerve cells.

overdose A deadly or toxic amount of drugs.

paranoia An unreasonable feeling of distrust. Thinking that everyone is out to get you.

prostitution The act of engaging in sexual relations for money.

purifying Mixing coca leaves with acid or kerosene to make cocaine powder.

stimulant Drug that speeds up the work of the body. Cocaine and crack are stimulants.

tolerance When the body becomes accustomed to a drug. With tolerance a body needs more and more of a drug to get the same high.

withdrawal Painful symptoms, such as chills, fever, trembling, cramps, or convulsions, that occur when an addict stops using a drug.

Where to Go for Help

In United States
Co-Anon Family Groups
P.O. Box 12124
Tucson, AZ 85732-2124
(520) 513-5028
Web site: http://www.co-anon.org

Cocaine Anonymous (CA)
World Service Office
3740 Overland Ave., Suite C
Los Angeles, CA 90034
(310) 559-5833
National Referral Hotline
(800) 347-8998
Web site: http://www.ca.org

Cocaine Hotline
Phoenix House
164 West 74th Street
New York, NY 10023
(800) COCAINE (262-2463)

In Canada
Al-Anon Family Groups
Capital Corporate Center
9 Antares Drive, Suite 245
Nepean, ON K2E 7V5
(613) 723-8484

World Directory Meeting Line
(800) 443-4525
Meeting Information Across Canada
(888) 425-2666
Web site: http://www.al-anon.alateen.org

Canadian Center on Substance Abuse
75 Albert Street, Suite 300
Ottawa, ON K1P 5E7
(613) 235-4048

Harvest House
Drug Rehabilitation Center for Teens
4406 River Road
Gloucester, ON K1V 1G1
(613) 822-1158
Web site: http://www.harvesthouse.org

Web Sites
Drug Education and Awareness
for Life
A Canadian-based Web site dedicated to informing young people about the dangers of drugs.
http://www.deal.org

Free Vibe
A Web site for teens with information about, and ways to stay off, of drugs.
http://www.freevibe.com

For Further Reading

Anonymous. *Go Ask Alice*. Old Tappan, NJ: Simon & Schuster Children's, 1998.

Chiu, Christina. *Teen Guide to Staying Sober*. Rev. ed. New York: Rosen Publishing Group, 1998.

Glass, George. *Drugs & Fitting In*. New York: Rosen Publishing Group, 1998.

Grosshandler-Smith, Janet. *Drugs & the Law*. Rev. ed. New York: Rosen Publishing Group, 1997.

Heuer, Marti. *Teen Addiction*. New York: Ballentine Books, Inc., 1997.

Hicks, John. *Drug Addiction: No Way I'm an Addict*. Brookfield, CT: Millbrook Press, 1997.

Huard, Donald. *Teen-Agers: What Will Cigarettes, Booze, "Safe Sex," and Drugs Do To You?* Prescott, AZ: Huard Publications, 1997.

Smith McLaughlin, Miriam, and Sandra Peyser Hazouri. *Addiction: The High That Brings You Down.* Springfield, NJ: Enslow Publishers, Inc., 1997.

Winters, Paul. *Teen Addiction.* San Diego, CA: Greenhaven Press, Inc., 1997.

Index

63

64 | About the Author

Rodney G. Peck is a graduate of Central Michigan University. He worked with the America's PRIDE program in drug prevention and education for four years. He then joined the Peace Corps in Belize, Central America, where he was assigned to a drug education program for two years. His work in drug prevention (especially with young people) has taken him to Canada, the U.S. Virgin Islands, and throughout the United States. Rodney is currently living in Memphis, Tennessee, pursuing an acting career. He continues to stay informed and to talk about the dangers of drugs.

Photo Credits

Cover photo © SuperStock; pp. 2, 6, 12, 17, 20, 22, 27, 46 by Stuart Rabinowitz; pp 30, 35, 38, 42 © AP/Wide World Photos; p. 50 by Stephanie FitzGerald.